Great Historic Debates and Speeches ™

THE LINCOLN-DOUGLAS SENATORIAL DEBATES OF 1858

A PRIMARY ❧ SOURCE ❧ INVESTIGATION

Jason Porterfield

rosen central
Primary Source ™

The Rosen Publishing Group, Inc., New York

Published in 2005 by The Rosen Publishing Group, Inc.
29 East 21st Street, New York, NY 10010

Unless otherwise attributed, all quotes in this book are excerpted from the official texts of the debates.

Library of Congress Cataloging-in-Publication Data

Porterfield, Jason.
The Lincoln-Douglas senatorial debates of 1858 : a primary source investigation / by Jason Porterfield. — 1st ed.
        p. cm. — (Great historic debates and speeches)
Includes bibliographical references (p.) and index.
ISBN 1-4042-0153-X (lib. bdg.)
1. Lincoln-Douglas debates, 1858—Juvenile literature. 2. Lincoln, Abraham, 1809–1865—Juvenile literature. 3. Douglas, Stephen Arnold, 1813–1861—Juvenile literature. 4. Lincoln, Abraham, 1809–1865—Quotations—Juvenile literature.
5. Douglas, Stephen Arnold, 1813–1861—Quotations—Juvenile literature.
[1. Lincoln-Douglas debates, 1858. 2. Lincoln, Abraham, 1809–1865. 3. Douglas, Stephen Arnold, 1813–1861.]
I. Title. II. Series.
E457.4.P68 2004
326'.0973—dc22

                                                                            2003025408

Manufactured in the United States of America

Cover images: Left: Photograph of Abraham Lincoln. Right: Photograph of Stephen Douglas.

CONTENTS

Abraham Lincoln gained a national reputation from his debates with Stephen Douglas. This photograph was taken by Mathew B. Brady on February 27, 1860, before Lincoln delivered a major political address in New York City.

Stephen Douglas served two years as a judge in the Supreme Court of Illinois and four years as a United States representative before he was elected to the Senate in 1847. This photograph of Douglas was taken sometime between 1855 and 1861.

INTRODUCTION

Slavery existed legally in what would become the United States for more than 200 years. Even as public sentiment shifted against it and Northern states banned slavery, the government continued to make compromises that allowed it to continue in some parts of the country. The compromises held the nation together. Yet they divided Americans into pro-slavery and antislavery factions.

Over time, the question of slavery became a major issue in elections. In 1858, in Illinois, an antislavery lawyer named Abraham Lincoln ran for the U.S. Senate against the pro-slavery incumbent Stephen Douglas. Over a series of seven historic debates, the two candidates argued about the future of slavery. Newspapers across the country publicized the Lincoln-Douglas debates. The encounters between the two candidates made history as the nation's first truly public argument over slavery. Ultimately, the debates played a crucial role in Lincoln's success in the 1860 presidential election, which led to the beginning of the Civil War. Although Lincoln did not call for the abolition of slavery during the debates, after he became president he began the process of ending slavery with his Emancipation Proclamation.

Today the Lincoln-Douglas debates are recognized for changing the way political campaigns unfold. They are highly regarded as examples of how to frame arguments and deliver them persuasively.

CHAPTER 1

A HOUSE DIVIDED

During the 1850s, the United States entered a period of great turmoil. The country was bitterly divided between slaveholders in the South and antislavery abolitionists in the North. Both sides wanted the country's laws to support their own positions. A series of compromises in Congress had held the nation together, but growing tensions between the two sides threatened the country's future.

Years of Compromise

The place of slavery in American society had been in question since the early days of the nation. The first blacks in Britain's North American colonies came as indentured servants, not as slaves. They arrived in Virginia in 1619 with the understanding that they would work for a period of time—usually seven years—to pay off the cost of the voyage. After the agreed-upon time had passed, they gained their freedom and usually land or clothing as "freedom dues."

Gradually, the system of indentured servitude changed. It was replaced by "slave codes" throughout the colonies. These laws made the servitude of blacks permanent and hereditary. This meant that the children of slaves were born into slavery.

By the time the Revolutionary War began in 1775, there were about 500,000 African Americans living in colonial America. All but 25,000 of them were enslaved. During the war, 5,000 African Americans served in the Continental army in exchange for their freedom. Moreover, many slave owners and states began freeing slaves in the spirit of independence for all. By the time the first census was taken in 1790, the number of free African Americans had risen to 60,000.

States throughout the North began passing laws to end or phase out slavery, though stiff opposition existed in parts of New York, Rhode Island, and New Jersey. Vermont became the first state to end slavery in 1777. The Northwest Ordinance, a bill passed by Congress in 1787 to govern new territories, barred slavery in the Northwest Territory, consisting of present-day Ohio, Indiana, Illinois, Michigan, and Wisconsin.

Though the importation of slaves from Africa became illegal in 1808, slavery remained an institution in the Southern states. This was primarily because local economies in the South were driven by agriculture rather than industry. Large plantations grew cotton, the nation's most valuable export at the time, and the growing and harvesting of cotton required a huge labor force. It was much cheaper for Southern planters to use slaves rather than hired workers to plant, harvest, and prepare cotton for sale.

Until 1818, there was a balance between slave states and free states in the country, with eleven of each guaranteeing equal representation in the Senate. That year, Missouri applied for statehood as a slave state, which threatened to upset the balance. Congress maintained the balance by admitting Maine as a free state in 1820. Before Missouri officially became a state, Congress added a condition known as the Missouri Compromise, which outlawed slavery north of 36 degrees, 30 minutes

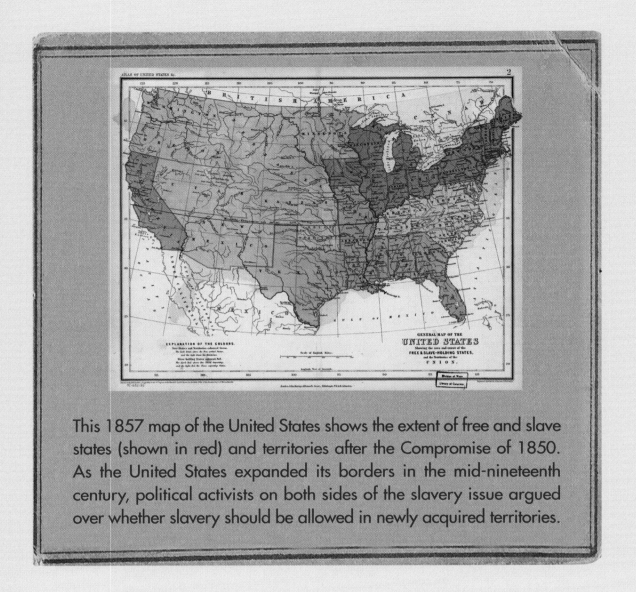

This 1857 map of the United States shows the extent of free and slave states (shown in red) and territories after the Compromise of 1850. As the United States expanded its borders in the mid-nineteenth century, political activists on both sides of the slavery issue argued over whether slavery should be allowed in newly acquired territories.

latitude. This piece of legislation governed the admittance of states for the next thirty years.

Meanwhile, freed African Americans and other opponents of slavery in the Northern states began calling for the federal government to abolish slavery in all states. These abolitionists, whose leaders included publisher William Lloyd Garrison and a former slave turned writer and public speaker named Frederick Douglass, grew increasingly vocal.

The balance between free states and slave states was once again threatened after the United States acquired territories from Mexico. Congress passed the Compromise of 1850 in an attempt to satisfy the demands of both free states and slave states. The Compromise of 1850 opened settlement of the Utah and Oklahoma Territories to slaveholders and admitted California as a free state. It included a provision for a Fugitive Slave Act that allowed Southern slaveholders to hunt down and reclaim slaves who had escaped to the North. Ultimately, the Compromise of 1850 succeeded only in increasing tensions between abolitionists and slaveholders.

The Little Giant

One of the architects of the Compromise of 1850 was Stephen Douglas, a senator from Illinois. Born in Vermont in 1813, Douglas first rose to prominence as a lawyer in Illinois. He served as a judge of the Illinois Supreme Court from 1841 to 1843, when he was elected to the U.S. House of Representatives. As a member of Congress, Douglas quickly made a name for himself as an advocate for American expansion in the West. He won the nickname the Little Giant for his small stature and his tremendous skills as an orator.

Douglas became a senator in 1847. He headed the Senate Committee on Territories, which regulated the entrance of states into the Union. Douglas supported a middle ground on the slavery issue. He opposed federal laws restricting or banning slavery in favor of "popular sovereignty." This approach allowed people living in the West to decide for themselves if they wanted to become free states or slave states.

Douglas's idea of popular sovereignty rose to the forefront of national politics in 1854, when he proposed legislation for the creation of the Kansas and Nebraska Territory. This Kansas-Nebraska Act repealed the part of the Missouri Compromise that restricted the spread of slavery north of the Missouri Compromise line. Instead, people would vote on legalizing slavery in their territories. In a speech to

THE LITTLE GIANT..IN THE CHARACTER OF THE GLADIATOR.

Throughout the 1840s and 1850s, Stephen Douglas was a power-house in American politics, especially within the Democratic Party. The illustration at left portrays him as a gladiator. It captures his fearless advocacy and defense of his doctrine of popular sovereignty, which proposed that the people of each new state should decide whether slavery would be allowed. The photograph at right was taken sometime between 1844 and 1860.

Congress on January 30, 1854, Douglas explained that "the legal effect of this is neither to legislate slavery into these territories nor out of them, but to leave the people do as they please. If they wish slavery, they have a right to it. If they do not want it, they will not have it, and you should not force it upon them."

The Kansas-Nebraska Act was passed in Congress and became law on May 30, 1854. However, instead of resolving the slavery issue peacefully, the Kansas-Nebraska Act opened the door for bloody border clashes between Kansas and Missouri. Slavery supporters poured across the border from Missouri, hoping to make Kansas a slave state.

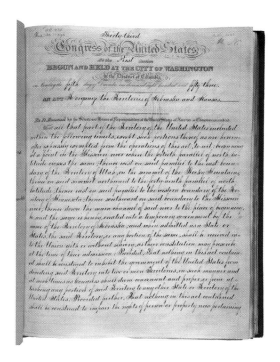

This is the first page of the Kansas-Nebraska Act of 1854. Kansas became known as "bleeding Kansas" in the aftermath of the act's passage because of the violence that erupted between antislavery and pro-slavery settlers over the question of whether slavery should be allowed.

The glaring shortcomings of the Kansas-Nebraska Act and the criticisms that Douglas faced because of them would come to haunt him during his campaign for reelection in 1858. Douglas faced unexpected competition for his Senate seat. As his reelection campaign began, he found himself opposed by a lawyer named Abraham Lincoln.

Honest Abe

Abraham Lincoln was born into a poor Kentucky family on February 12, 1809. The self-taught Lincoln moved to New Salem, Illinois, in 1831, where he became popular for his storytelling abilities and gained a reputation for being a man of integrity and strong character. Those familiar with his easygoing and forthright manner called him Honest Abe.

Before entering politics, Lincoln worked as a grocer and a surveyor, finally resorting to splitting rails (wood for fences), among other odd jobs. He was elected to the state legislature in 1834 as a member of the Whig Party. Two years later, he earned his license to practice law. He went into private practice after leaving his seat in the legislature in 1841.

At top is a photograph of Abraham Lincoln, taken around 1847 when Lincoln was a congressman. At bottom is an 1846 Whig campaign handbill showing the party's slate of candidates, led by Lincoln, for the Seventh Congressional District of Illinois.

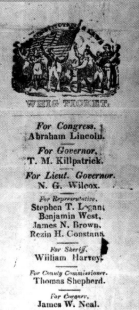

WHIG TICKET.

For Congress.
Abraham Lincoln.

For Governor,
T. M. Killpatrick.

For Lieut. Governor.
N. G. Wilcox.

For Representative.
Stephen T. Logan,
Benjamin West,
James N. Brown,
Rezin H. Constant.

For Sheriff.
William Harvey.

For County Commissioner.
Thomas Shepherd.

For Coroner.
James W. Neal.

For a Convention.

In 1847, Lincoln was elected to the U.S. House of Representatives. The young congressman soon gained a reputation for speaking out against slavery and the Mexican-American War (1846–1848). (He had become a vigorous opponent of slavery after witnessing a slave auction in New Orleans just before moving to Illinois.) Opting not to run for reelection in 1849, Lincoln returned to practicing law. He did not remain out of the public eye for long, emerging in 1854 to protest the Kansas-Nebraska Act.

When the Whig Party dissolved in 1856, Lincoln joined the new Republican Party. His antislavery convictions were further galvanized in 1857, when the Supreme Court ruled on the *Dred Scott v. Sanford* case. The *Dred Scott* decision declared unconstitutional any law regulating slavery in the territories or prohibiting a slave owner from taking slaves into a territory. Lincoln made several public speaking appearances, condemning both the Kansas-Nebraska Act and the Dred Scott decision. Republican Party leaders took notice of his energy and speaking abilities and nominated him to oppose Stephen Douglas in the 1858 Senate campaign. In his acceptance speech, given in Springfield, Illinois, on June 16, 1858, Lincoln declared,

"A house divided against itself cannot stand." I believe this government cannot endure, permanently half slave and half free. I do not expect the Union to be dissolved—I do not expect the house to fall—but I do expect it will cease to be divided. It will become all one thing, or all the other.

Lincoln's Challenge

Douglas did not consider Abraham Lincoln to be a serious opponent. Despite Lincoln's single term in the U.S. House of Representatives

POLITICAL PARTIES

The two major political parties in 1858 were the Democrats and the Republicans. Before the Republican Party formed in 1854, the Democrats competed with the Whig Party for control of the government. The Whigs fell into disarray after the Kansas-Nebraska Act passed in 1854.

Antislavery Whigs and Democrats united to form the core of the new Republican Party. Some people also joined from other parties, such as the Free Soil Party, which advocated the free distribution of public lands, and the Know-Nothing Party, whose members discriminated against immigrants. Somehow, these very different groups stuck together to form an antislavery party.

and his recent speeches, Douglas was confident that his being the better known of the two candidates would guarantee his victory. But the determined Lincoln soon developed a campaign tactic that used Douglas's fame to his disadvantage. As Douglas traveled throughout Illinois giving speeches, Lincoln followed and spoke the next day, usually to the same audience that Douglas had addressed the day before. Newspapers supporting Douglas began ridiculing Lincoln. The *Chicago Times* mockingly suggested that he join with one of "two very good circuses and menageries traveling through the State; these exhibitions always draw good crowds at country towns."

Instead, Lincoln challenged Douglas to a series of debates. Douglas's initial impulse was to decline. The debates could only help his opponent gain public recognition. However, he realized that refusing the challenge would open him up to charges of cowardice. Eventually, the candidates agreed to meet seven times, once in each congressional district of Illinois. One would speak first for an hour. The other would have an hour to reply. Then the first speaker would give a one-hour response. The schedule slightly favored Douglas, allowing him to make the opening and closing remarks four times. Regardless, Lincoln was satisfied with getting this chance to properly address the issues before the people.

CHAPTER 2

DOUGLAS DEFENDS HIS RECORD

L incoln and Douglas scheduled their seven debates in Illinois for the final months of the Senate race. The two candidates planned to appear in towns where they had not yet spoken during the campaign. They faced each other in Ottawa on August 21, 1858, Freeport on August 27, Jonesboro on September 15, Charleston on September 18, Galesburg on October 7, Quincy on October 13, and Alton on October 15.

Ottawa

The crowd at the first debate in the Ottawa town square was large and boisterous. Ten thousand people gathered in this town of 9,000 to watch the debate, including military units in full-dress uniform and marching bands. Both candidates had supporters present who cheered their favorite and jeered the opponent.

Stephen Douglas spoke first in Ottawa. Annoyed with having to debate Lincoln at all, the Little Giant sought to bury his opponent early. As the main theme of his opening

Springfield, July 31. 1858.

Hon. S. A. Douglas.
    Dear Sir

        Yours of yesterday, naming places, times, and terms, for joint discussion between us, was received this morning— Although, by the terms, as you propose, you take four openings and closes to my _three_, I accede, and thus close the arrangement— I direct this to you at Hillsboro; and shall try to have both your letter and this, appear in the Journal and Register of monday, morning—

                    Your Obt. Servt.
                    A. Lincoln—

In this July 31, 1858, letter from Abraham Lincoln to Stephen Douglas, Lincoln agrees to the terms of the debates. He writes, "Although, by the terms, as you propose, you take four openings and closes to my three, I accede." Lincoln was willing to accept these terms because he recognized the potential value of the debates to boosting his stature during the campaign.

speech and one of his major speaking points throughout the debates, Douglas accused Lincoln of trying to subvert the Democratic and Whig Parties, contributing to the demise of the Whig Party in 1856. He asserted that Lincoln's goal was to "dissolve the old Whig party on the one hand, and to dissolve the old Democratic party on the other, and to connect the members of both into an Abolition party, under the name and disguise of the Republican party."

Douglas read from a radical antislavery document that he claimed the Republicans had adopted at an 1854 convention. The senator accused Lincoln of wholeheartedly endorsing the resolutions making up the platform. He next fired questions relating to the resolutions at Lincoln. Douglas demanded to know if Lincoln still wanted the Fugitive Slave Act repealed, if he wished to end interstate slave trade and the slave trade in Washington, D.C., and if he desired a ban on slavery in all national territories.

Douglas intended another question to cast doubt on whether Lincoln was keeping the wishes and best interests of the people in mind. "I want to know whether he stands pledged against the admission of a new State into the Union with such a Constitution as the people of that State may see fit to make," thundered Douglas. Responding to his own question, Douglas evoked the founding fathers to demonstrate that it was he, not Lincoln, who followed in the footsteps of the framers of the Declaration of Independence and the Constitution:

> This doctrine of Mr. Lincoln, of uniformity among the institutions of the different States, is a new doctrine, never dreamed of by Washington, Madison, or the framers of this Government. Mr. Lincoln and the Republican party set themselves up as wiser than these men who made this Government, which has flourished for

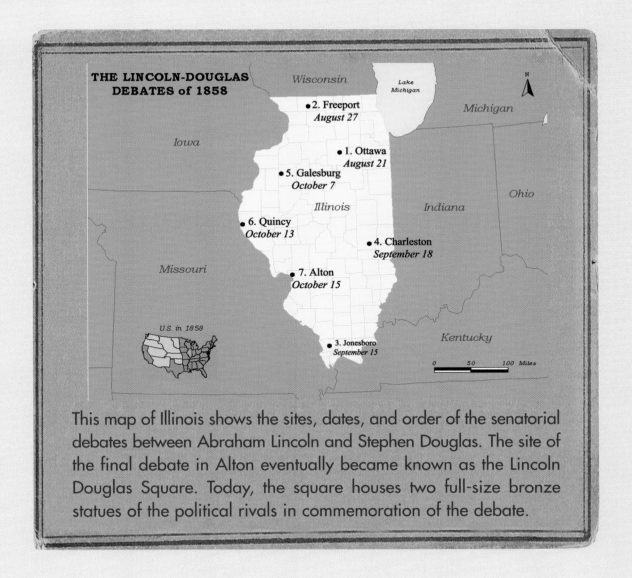

THE LINCOLN-DOUGLAS
DEBATES of 1858

Wisconsin

Lake Michigan

Michigan

Iowa

● 2. Freeport
August 27

● 1. Ottawa
August 21

● 5. Galesburg
October 7

Illinois

Indiana

Ohio

● 6. Quincy
October 13

● 4. Charleston
September 18

Missouri

● 7. Alton
October 15

U.S. in 1858

● 3. Jonesboro
September 15

Kentucky

0   50   100 *Miles*

This map of Illinois shows the sites, dates, and order of the senatorial debates between Abraham Lincoln and Stephen Douglas. The site of the final debate in Alton eventually became known as the Lincoln Douglas Square. Today, the square houses two full-size bronze statues of the political rivals in commemoration of the debate.

seventy years under the principle of popular sovereignty, recognizing the right of each State to do as it pleased . . . I believe that this new doctrine preached by Mr. Lincoln and his party will dissolve the Union if it succeeds. They are trying to array all the Northern States in one body against the South, to excite a sectional war between the free States and the slave States, in order that the one or the other may be driven to the wall.

Douglas left the first debate triumphant. His supporters crowded around him as he departed, cheering and shouting. Lincoln had seemed entirely flummoxed by Douglas's questions and stumbled in replying. The Little Giant had every reason to feel confident on the road to Freeport.

Freeport and Jonesboro

As with the debates that followed, the scene in Freeport closely resembled the spectacle in Ottawa, with large crowds and loud supporters on both sides. This time, Douglas had to wait for Lincoln to speak first.

Douglas did not carry the Freeport debate as easily as he had carried the one in Ottawa. Lincoln, cool and confident, put forth four questions for Douglas to answer. The second addressed whether people in a territory had the right to ban slavery if they wished. Douglas replied in a habitual defense of his idea of popular sovereignty:

> I answer emphatically, as Mr. Lincoln has heard me answer a hundred times from every stump in Illinois, that in my opinion the people of a Territory can, by lawful means, exclude slavery from their limits prior to the formation of a State Constitution . . . It matters not what way the Supreme Court may hereafter decide as to the abstract question whether slavery may or may not go into a Territory under the Constitution, the people have the lawful means to introduce it or exclude it as they please, for the reason that slavery cannot exist a day or an hour anywhere, unless it is supported by local police regulations.

Douglas's reply became known as the Freeport Doctrine and precisely outlined his beliefs. People in the territories should be able to decide the

James Buchanan was the fifteenth president of the United States. He served one term between 1857 and 1861. His rift with Stephen Douglas over how to resolve a dispute about slavery in Kansas hurt his chances for reelection. He is the only unmarried president in United States history.

slavery issue for themselves. Without the support of the people, local authorities would have difficulties in enforcing the law, whether pro-slavery or antislavery. His tone in replying to Lincoln indicated frustration with the question. He accused Lincoln of dodging his questions. He also criticized Lincoln's opposition to the Mexican-American War, fought between the United States and Mexico after a long dispute over national borders.

Douglas received a frosty welcome in Jonesboro. Located in southern Illinois, most of its residents were Democrats. But they supported President James Buchanan, with whom Douglas had a running feud.

An anti-slavery Democrat, Lyman Trumbull was elected to the United States House of Representatives in 1854, then was appointed to the Senate in 1855. Before his congressional career, Trumbull was the Illinois secretary of state, a member of the Illinois legislature, and an Illinois Supreme Court justice.

Only 2,000 people came out to see this debate, the smallest crowd present throughout the series.

This time, Douglas reiterated his charges of an abolitionist conspiracy backing the Republican Party. Replying to a question posed by Lincoln regarding whether or not he would help pass legislation to protect slavery, Douglas repeated his stance that the government should not interfere. He said, "I answer him that it is a fundamental article in the Democratic creed that there should be non-interference and non-intervention by Congress with slavery in the States or territories."

Charleston, Galesburg, Quincy, and Alton

The candidates entered Charleston for the fourth debate on September 18. The Little Giant became frustrated by Lincoln's repeated assertions that he was involved in a conspiracy to spread slavery to Kansas. He lashed out, denouncing Lincoln's evidence as having been concocted by another Illinois senator, Lyman Trumbull. "Why, I

This illustration, published in *McClure's Magazine* in 1858, depicts the fifth debate between Abraham Lincoln and Stephen Douglas in Galesburg on October 7, 1858. The caption that accompanied the image noted that the "platform from which they spoke was erected at the east end of Knox College. The students took a lively interest in the contest, decorating the college gayly with flags and streamers."

THE LECOMPTON CONSTITUTION

The debate over slavery in the territories became extremely heated in Kansas. The pro-slavery and antislavery sides grew so far apart that each side drew up a state constitution. The pro-slavery side failed to pass its so-called Lecompton Constitution, which would have allowed slavery. President James Buchanan urged Congress to accept the Lecompton Constitution, even though Kansas voters had rejected it. Stephen Douglas felt Buchanan was trying to ignore the will of the people, violating their popular sovereignty. He openly criticized Buchanan's position. The rift that grew between them remained until Buchanan left office.

ask, does not Mr. Lincoln make a speech of his own instead of taking up his time reading Trumbull's speech?" Douglas wondered. "He has several times charged that the Supreme Court, President Pierce, President Buchanan and myself, at the time I introduced the Nebraska bill in January, 1854, at Washington, entered into a conspiracy to establish slavery all over this country," Douglas told the crowd. He offered his record on the Compromise of 1850 and his ideas about popular sovereignty as evidence to the contrary.

By the fifth debate in Galesburg, the strain of debating began to show on Stephen Douglas. Speaking in a hoarse voice, Douglas again outlined his positions on popular sovereignty. He accused Lincoln of changing his political views as the debates moved southward. "My

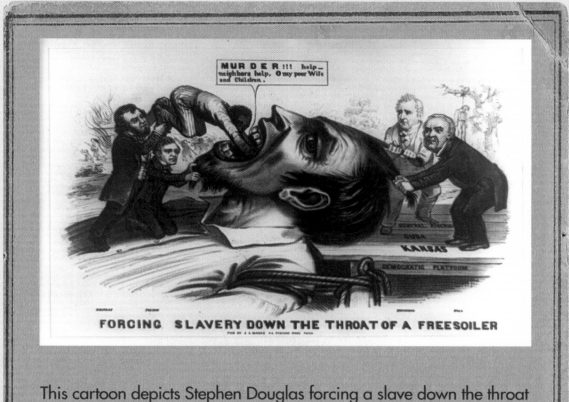

MURDER !!! help— neighbors help, O my poor Wife and Children.

FORCING SLAVERY DOWN THE THROAT OF A FREESOILER

This cartoon depicts Stephen Douglas forcing a slave down the throat of a Free Soiler as other prominent Democratic politicians restrain the Free Soiler. The Free Soil Party was made up of antislavery activists who opposed the Kansas-Nebraska Act.

friend Lincoln finds it's extremely difficult to manage a debate in the centre part of the State, where there is a mixture of men from the North and the South," he declared, to much laughter from his supporters.

The debates at Quincy a week later were especially heated. Douglas responded to Lincoln's attacks on the *Dred Scott* decision, accusing his opponent of "stimulating the passions of men to resort to violence and to mobs instead of to the law." Douglas urged listeners to turn away from the slavery question so that Americans could get on with growing and "filling up our prairies, clearing our wildernesses and building cities, towns, railroads and other internal improvements, and thus make this the asylum of the oppressed of the whole earth."

Douglas opened the final debate at Alton on October 15. Looking tired and worn, he spoke in a voice so hoarse that he could hardly be heard through the first parts of his speech. This time he spent much of his time outlining his views on the governing of Kansas. He spoke mainly of his differences with Democratic president James Buchanan over the Lecompton Constitution. "I was opposed to that constitution because I did not believe that it was the act and deed of the people, but on the contrary, the act of a small, pitiful minority acting in the name of the majority," he said.

Douglas concluded his remarks, and the debates, with another defense of popular sovereignty: "All you have a right to ask is that the people shall do as they please; if they want slavery let them have it; if they do not want it, allow them to refuse to encourage it. My friends, if, as I have said before, we will only live up to this great fundamental principle there will be peace between the North and the South." He implored his audience to obey the Supreme Court, the Constitution, and the wishes of the founding fathers.

CHAPTER 3

LINCOLN PRESENTS AN ALTERNATIVE

Compared to Douglas, Abraham Lincoln was a political newcomer and virtually unknown. Before the debates, he had worked to publicize his campaign by placing articles about the Republican Party in newspapers throughout the state. As he prepared to reply to Douglas's opening remarks at the first debate in Ottawa, Lincoln knew he would have to use the debates to win the hearts and minds of the Illinois voters.

Ottawa

Though Lincoln had been the challenger, his reply to Douglas's opening remarks made it obvious that he was not comfortable in the debate format. Lincoln liked to plan and revise his speeches, rather than make a hastily arranged reply to meet his opponent's claims. Lincoln opened by denying the Republican Party platform that Douglas had read from. Lincoln went on to claim that his position on slavery was much more moderate than Douglas had alleged. As evidence, he read from a speech he had given at Peoria, Illinois, in 1854. There, he had acknowledged the difficulty of abolishing slavery:

> When it is said that the institution [slavery] exists, and that it is very difficult to get rid of it, in any satisfactory way, I can understand and appreciate the saying. I surely will not blame them for not doing what I should not know how to do myself. If all earthly power were given me, I should not know what to do, as to the existing institution.

For the most part, Lincoln dodged Douglas's questions and accusations. However, he spent much of his time denying Douglas's charges of his involvement in an abolitionist conspiracy. Speaking in obscure legal language and repeating worn jokes, Lincoln questioned Douglas's logic as a "fantastic arrangement of words, by which a man can prove a horse-chestnut to be a chestnut horse."

Lincoln was largely satisfied with his first debate appearance. Most of his supporters, however, felt he had been too cautious. "Don't act on the defensive at all," urged *Chicago Press and Tribune* editor Joseph Medill. "Don't refer to your past speeches or positions, . . . but hold Dug [Douglas] up as a traitor and conspirator a proslavery bamboozelling demogogue."

Freeport and Jonesboro

Lincoln seemed much more at ease speaking before the more abolition-friendly audience at Freeport. Honest Abe opened his remarks by replying to Douglas's questions from the first debate. His answers did not fit with the Little Giant's characterization of Lincoln as a radical abolitionist. Lincoln said he did not favor repealing the Fugitive Slave Act, did not wish to abolish slavery from Washington, D.C., and was

This illustration shows Abraham Lincoln addressing the audience during one of the 1858 senatorial debates with Stephen Douglas. Lincoln's performance and his political stature in Illinois grew as the debates progressed.

not necessarily against admitting more slave states or any state with whatever sort of constitution its people wanted to make. He did, however, oppose permitting the spread of slavery into the territories. "I am impliedly, if not expressly, pledged to a belief in the right and duty of Congress to prohibit slavery in all the United States Territories," he said.

Lincoln also stated that he would not oppose admitting more slave states. But he did not believe any emerging states would really want to institute slavery if the precedent had not already been set:

If slavery shall be kept out of the Territories during the territorial existence of any one given Territory, and then the people shall, having a fair chance and a clear field, when they come to adopt the Constitution, do such an extraordinary thing as to adopt a Slave Constitution, uninfluenced by the actual presence of the institution among them, I see no alternative, if we own the country, but to admit them into the Union.

Lincoln then put forth four questions to Douglas. The second was the most important and the boldest step Lincoln made throughout the debate. He asked Douglas if the people living in a territory had the right to "exclude slavery from its limits prior to the formation of a State Constitution?" If Douglas answered no, then Lincoln could claim that Douglas was not sincere about supporting popular sovereignty. Douglas answered yes, potentially upsetting people who wanted slavery to spread.

Lincoln again turned to the subject of the resolutions that Douglas had read from in Ottawa and accused Lincoln of supporting. He informed the crowd that the doctrine had never even been adopted by Republicans in Springfield. While doing so, he questioned Douglas's honesty and sense of fair play.

When the whole matter turns out as it does, and when we consider who Judge Douglas is—that he is a distinguished Senator of the United States—that he has served nearly twelve years as such—that his character is not at all limited as an ordinary Senator of the United States, but that his name has become of world-wide renown—it is most extraordinary that he should so far forget all the suggestions of justice to an adversary, or of prudence to himself, as to venture upon the assertion of that which the slightest investigation would have shown him to be wholly false.

By questioning both Douglas's stance on popular sovereignty and his reading of a false platform, Lincoln had successfully rattled his opponent. He could travel on to Jonesboro feeling more confident in his abilities.

Lincoln knew that the crowd at Jonesboro would be unfriendly toward him. Douglas attempted to bait Lincoln into endorsing racial equality for African Americans, a position favored by very few Americans at the time. Lincoln avoided the question and instead attacked the sincerity of Douglas's Freeport Doctrine. He did not believe that Douglas's proposals would truly keep slaves out of territories that voted to ban slavery.

Charleston, Galesburg, Quincy, and Alton

Lincoln opened his remarks at Charleston with a frank statement of his position on racial equality: "I am not, nor ever have been, in favor of bringing about in any way the social and political equality of the white and dark races." Lincoln's view was a common one even among abolitionists, many of whom had no interest in making African Americans "voters or jurors." Lincoln went on to charge Douglas with conspiring to bring slavery to Kansas, despite Douglas's disapproval of the Lecompton Constitution. Much of Lincoln's evidence came from Senator Lyman Trumbull, whom Douglas accused of making up evidence. Lincoln ultimately spent much of his remaining time defending Trumbull against Douglas's charges.

The fifth debate at Galesburg went much better for Lincoln. While Douglas's voice began failing him, Lincoln's rang loud and

THE CAMPAIGN IN ILLINOIS.

THE LAST JOINT DEBATE.

DOUGLAS AND LINCOLN AT ALTON.

5,000 TO 10,000 PERSONS PRESENT!

LINCOLN AGAIN REFUSES TO ANSWER WHETHER HE WILL VOTE TO ADMIT KANSAS IF HER PEOPLE APPLY WITH A CONSTITUTION RECOGNIZING SLAVERY.

APPEARS IN HIS OLD CHARACTER OF THE "ARTFUL DODGER."

TRIES TO PALM HIMSELF OFF TO THE WHIGS OF MADISON COUNTY AS A FRIEND OF HENRY CLAY AND NO ABOLITIONIST, AND IS EXPOSED!!

GREAT SPEECHES OF SENATOR DOUGLAS.

This anti-Lincoln poster addresses the final debate between Abraham Lincoln and Stephen Douglas. It refers to Lincoln as an "Artful Dodger" and accuses him of refusing to answer whether he would support statehood for Kansas if it adopted a pro-slavery constitution. The poster notes that between 6,000 and 10,000 people attended this debate.

clear. He affirmed that, though he did not believe in racial equality, he felt that African Americans were entitled to life, liberty, and the pursuit of happiness as offered by the Declaration of Independence.

I believe the entire records of the world, from the date of the Declaration of Independence up to within three years ago, may be searched in vain for one single affirmation, from one single man, that the negro was not included in the Declaration of Independence.

SENATOR LYMAN TRUMBULL

Lyman Trumbull had been elected as an Illinois senator in 1855. At the time, he belonged to the Democratic Party. Shortly after his election, Trumbull joined the Republicans. The political switch prompted Douglas's suspicions that he and Lincoln—a former Whig—were trying to bring the two traditional political parties over to the abolitionist side. Later in his career, Trumbull would help pass legislation ending slavery in the United States. Trumbull cheerfully described himself as "willing to be radical lawfully."

Lincoln accused Douglas of trying to turn public sentiment against granting African Americans basic human rights. Douglas, he said, was in "every possible way preparing the public mind, by his vast influence, for making the institution of slavery perpetual and national."

At the sixth debate in Quincy, Lincoln reminded the audience of the chief difference between himself and Senator Douglas. He described the pro-slavery position of the Democratic Party and the antislavery stand taken by Republicans. Lincoln spoke of Douglas as a leading Democrat who had the "high distinction, so far as I know, of never having said slavery is either right or wrong." The remark made Douglas appear cowardly for not stating his own beliefs. Lincoln, however, had frequently spoken of his antislavery feelings.

Lincoln reserved his strongest statement for the seventh and final debate at Alton. He again repeated his denial of Douglas's charges that he and the Republican Party were involved in a conspiracy against the slave states. Speaking before a crowd that largely sympathized with slaveholders, he reminded them that the question of whether slavery was right or wrong would not go away. No matter how much they and Stephen Douglas may wish to ignore it, the nation would someday have to solve the problem of what to do about slavery.

> It is the eternal struggle between these two principles—right and wrong—throughout the world. They are the two principles that have stood face to face from the beginning of time; and will ever continue to struggle. The one is the common right of humanity and the other the divine right of kings.

CHAPTER 4

TO THE WHITE HOUSE

Thousands of Illinois residents had greeted Lincoln and Douglas at every stop during the course of the debates. Civic organizations, local politicians, even entire families showed up, hoping to lend support to their favorite candidate. Yet they were not the only ones to witness the debates. Newspapers from all over the country sent reporters to cover the story, often coloring their accounts to fit the politics of the editors. Thus, the entire United States population witnessed the struggle between the two politicians as they engaged in the country's most public argument yet over slavery.

The Senate Election

At the time of the Lincoln-Douglas debates, Senate elections were very different from the way they are today. Voters at that time did not directly cast their ballots for senators. Instead, they voted only for members of the state legislature. The state legislature then selected the senators who would represent the state in the U.S. Senate. If voters supported a

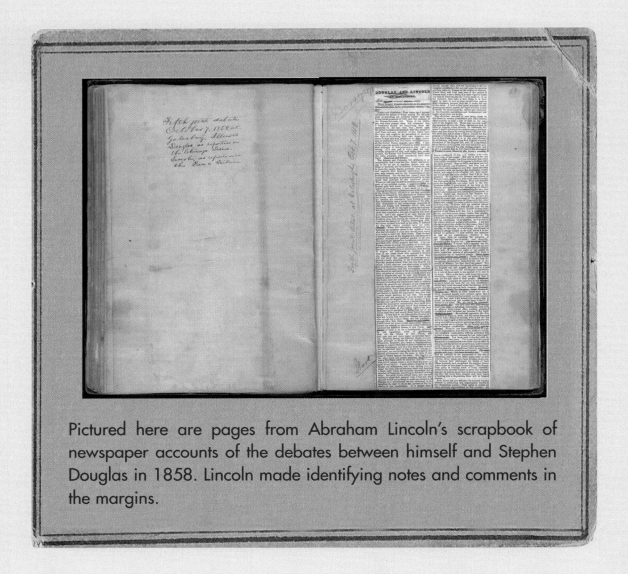

Pictured here are pages from Abraham Lincoln's scrapbook of newspaper accounts of the debates between himself and Stephen Douglas in 1858. Lincoln made identifying notes and comments in the margins.

particular candidate for the Senate, they chose legislators from his political party. The party that held the majority in the state legislature controlled the selection of the senator.

The race between Abraham Lincoln and Stephen Douglas was very close. Both speakers performed well in the debates, with Douglas outperforming Lincoln early on before Lincoln grew comfortable with the format. Many of their speeches repeated points covered earlier. Both discussed many topics that had little to do with the election, with Lincoln defending Senator Trumbull and Douglas explaining his differences from President Buchanan.

Voter turnout for the November 2, 1858, senatorial election in Illinois was greater than it had been for the 1856 presidential election. The rural counties in southern Illinois overwhelmingly voted for Democratic candidates. Republicans won in the more urban, northern parts of the state. Republican candidates won more popular votes but did not gain enough seats to elect Lincoln. The final balloting gave Douglas fifty-four legislature votes to Lincoln's forty-six, good enough to reelect Douglas for another six years.

Lincoln was disappointed but not surprised by the outcome. Though he felt his political career was over, he had no regrets about challenging Douglas. As he wrote to his friend Anson G. Henry on November 19, 1858, he was at least glad of getting the chance to share his views on slavery:

> I am glad I made the late race. It gave me a hearing on the great and durable question of the age, which I could have had in no other way; and though I now sink out of view, and shall be forgotten, I believe I have made some marks which will tell for the cause of civil liberty long after I am gone.

The Republican Leader and the Senator

Abraham Lincoln's belief that he would fade into obscurity soon proved false. Despite his election loss, Lincoln emerged as the most prominent Republican in Illinois. He felt a responsibility to help the party win the presidential election in 1860.

Though he had won the Senate race, Stephen Douglas's political career suffered after the debates. The Freeport Doctrine alienated many

Southern Democrats, who felt that he was no longer committed to their support of slavery. The Democratic leadership in the Senate removed Douglas from the chairmanship of the Committee on Territories, a dramatic turnaround for a man who had been the party's favorite to receive the presidential nomination in 1860.

Rather than dwell on his declining popularity, Douglas began working to bring Republican voters to his side. He pointed out that he had opposed laws that would protect slavery in the territories and reopen the African slave trade. Douglas cited popular sovereignty as the best way to keep the nation intact. Allowing the territories to decide the slavery question for themselves would prevent the slaveholders from passing a nationwide slave code and the abolitionists from banning slavery altogether. He still hoped to become president by attracting moderate voters, ignoring the extremist slaveholders as well as abolitionists.

Lincoln viewed Douglas as a threat to the Republican Party's chances of winning the presidency. He began campaigning for the Republicans in Ohio, where Douglas was touring in 1859 to support Democratic candidates. Lincoln once again found himself following the advice of his friend Joseph Medill, who wrote in a letter: "As you are not a candidate you can talk out as boldly as you please . . . hit below the belt as well as above, and kick like thunder."

Though the two men did not face each other, they resumed addressing the issues of the debates during their campaigns. Douglas continued pushing his popular sovereignty plan to audiences. Lincoln voiced his belief that unless slavery was restricted, it would push into the territories. The territories, he believed, should be reserved for people looking to improve their conditions in life. Slavery within the territories would create an economic system in which workers would have difficulty competing with slave labor. He told his audiences, "it is

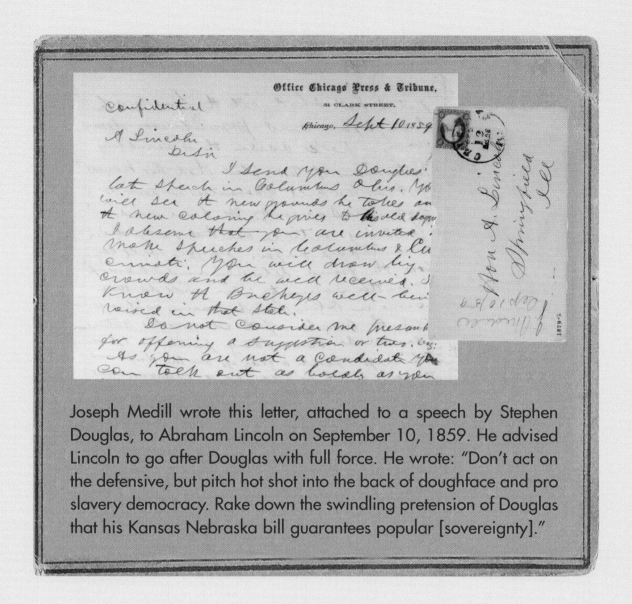

Joseph Medill wrote this letter, attached to a speech by Stephen Douglas, to Abraham Lincoln on September 10, 1859. He advised Lincoln to go after Douglas with full force. He wrote: "Don't act on the defensive, but pitch hot shot into the back of doughface and pro slavery democracy. Rake down the swindling pretension of Douglas that his Kansas Nebraska bill guarantees popular [sovereignty]."

due to yourselves as voters, as owners of the new territories, that you shall keep those territories free, in the best conditions for all such of your gallant sons as may choose to go there."

Audiences in the western states applauded Lincoln's speeches, and some people suggested that he run for president. Republican newspapers began endorsing him for either president or vice president. At first, Lincoln himself did not take the endorsements seriously. He had little formal education and few politically connected friends in the East. He had not held an office in ten years.

However, no strong Republican candidate emerged among the many seeking the party's nomination.

Lincoln began moving to strengthen his position as a possible Republican contender. He compiled and published his debates with Douglas into a single manuscript, using reports of his own speeches from the *Chicago Press and Tribune* and of Douglas's from the *Chicago Times*. The result was a 268-page volume titled *Political Debates Between Hon. Abraham Lincoln and Hon. Stephen A. Douglas, in the Celebrated Campaign of 1858, in Illinois*. The book came out in early 1860 and

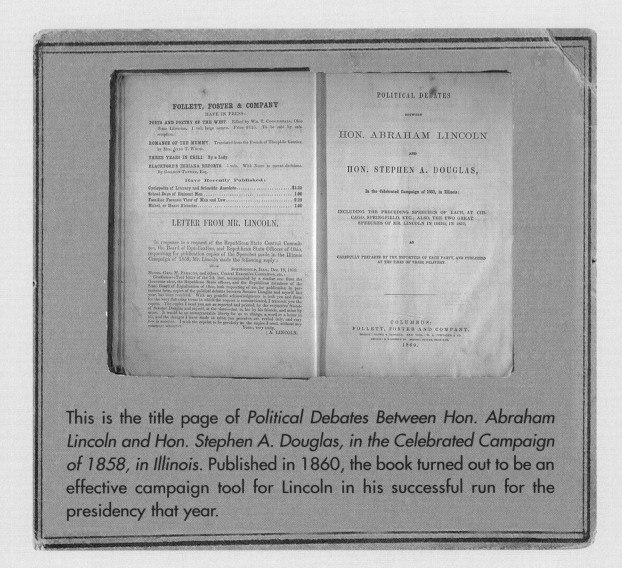

This is the title page of *Political Debates Between Hon. Abraham Lincoln and Hon. Stephen A. Douglas, in the Celebrated Campaign of 1858, in Illinois*. Published in 1860, the book turned out to be an effective campaign tool for Lincoln in his successful run for the presidency that year.

became a best-seller overnight. Readers who had not seen reports of all of the debates now had a chance to review the positions of two possible presidential candidates. By publishing the debates, Lincoln slyly distributed an account of his ideas and beliefs among the voting population.

Lincoln also expanded his speaking circuit to the eastern states. In February 1860, he accepted an invitation to speak at the abolitionist Henry Ward Beecher's Plymouth Church in Brooklyn, New York. The venue was later changed to the Cooper Union building in Manhattan. The event offered Lincoln a chance to impress an eastern audience with his speaking abilities and advocate his party's antislavery position. In what would soon become one of his most famous speeches, Lincoln denounced threats from the Southern states that they would secede from the Union if a Republican candidate became president. Lincoln asked his audience to resist efforts to expand slavery into the territories and to restrict it to the South. "Let us have faith that right makes might, and in that faith, let us, to the end, dare to do our duty as we understand it," he concluded.

Lincoln's speech helped him to gain ground on other Republican candidates. His position was antislavery enough to please abolitionists, yet his caution in not seeking a nationwide ban on slavery attracted many conservative former Whigs. Nonetheless, the question of whether or not he would win the nomination depended on his old rival, Stephen Douglas. Douglas was immensely popular in the West, and if he won the Democratic nomination, the Republican convention might also be inclined to choose a western candidate. Lincoln's advisors cultivated his image as a self-made frontiersman, until Lincoln's new nickname, the "Rail Splitter," became as well-known as the "Little Giant."

When it came time for the Republican Convention meeting in Chicago in May 1860 to choose a candidate, Lincoln was clearly a

A BRAWL IN THE HOUSE OF REPRESENTATIVES

Congress grew so tense over slavery that a massive fistfight broke out on March 23, 1858. Lawrence Keitt of South Carolina and Pennsylvania's Galusha Grow were debating slavery in the frontier when they exchanged insults. The pair soon came to blows. Within minutes, dozens of congressmen were attacking each other. The fight reached its peak when Grow tried to grab Mississippi congressman William Barksdale by the hair and instead pulled off his hairpiece. The brawl ended in general laughter.

serious contender. Westerners were attracted to the Rail Splitter's frontier image. Easterners and abolitionists reading printed copies of the Lincoln-Douglas debates and his Cooper Union speech accepted his antislavery position and vision for the nation. On May 18, 1860, at the Republican National Convention, the Republican Party chose Abraham Lincoln as its presidential candidate.

The Race for the White House

The nominating process did not go so well for Stephen Douglas. The Democratic National Convention, meeting in Charleston, South Carolina, on April 23, 1860, turned into a heated affair. The convention met for ten days, adjourned for six weeks, and then met again in Baltimore, Maryland, on June 18 for another six days.

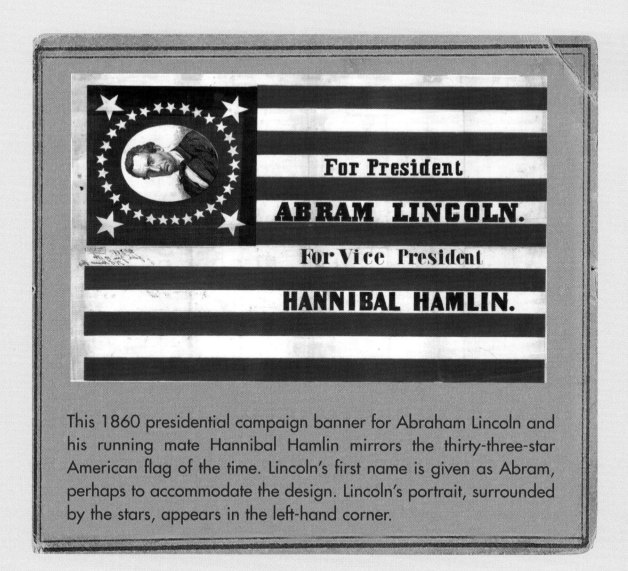

For President
ABRAM LINCOLN.

For Vice President
HANNIBAL HAMLIN.

This 1860 presidential campaign banner for Abraham Lincoln and his running mate Hannibal Hamlin mirrors the thirty-three-star American flag of the time. Lincoln's first name is given as Abram, perhaps to accommodate the design. Lincoln's portrait, surrounded by the stars, appears in the left-hand corner.

Pro-slavery delegates still did not trust Stephen Douglas. His Freeport Doctrine had angered many, as had statements he had made in the third debate against government intervention in protecting slavery. Though the party did not wholeheartedly favor him, Douglas had many supporters in the North and West. The Southern Democrats eventually stormed out of the convention, fracturing the party. The remaining delegates nominated Douglas to run against Lincoln. The delegates who left the convention nominated a candidate of their own, the pro-slavery vice president John C. Breckinridge.

CHAPTER 5

LINCOLN'S LEGACY

The three major candidates in the election of 1860 represented three opposing doctrines. Breckinridge wanted Congress to pass laws protecting slavery in the territories. Douglas still argued for popular sovereignty, allowing the territories to decide on slavery themselves, regardless of the *Dred Scott* decision that allowed slaveholders to take slaves with them into the frontier. Lincoln remained committed to keeping slavery out of the territories altogether. A fourth candidate named John Bell of the Constitutional Union Party held vaguely antislavery views. Though Lincoln did not get more than 50 percent of the vote, the fracturing of the Democratic Party helped him win the presidency.

Lincoln's election to the White House did not bode well for the fate of the Union. Days after his election, South Carolina formed a convention to debate secession from the United States. Other states in the South followed suit. Some in the North were willing to allow the states to leave peacefully. Others thought a compromise could be hastily drawn to keep the United States together.

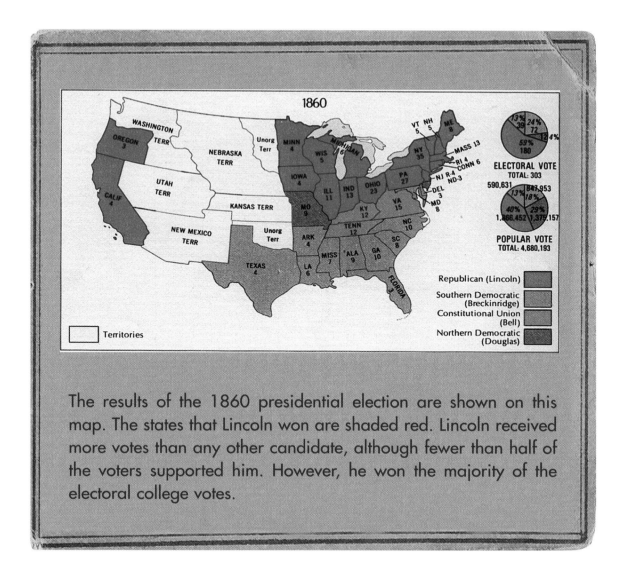

The results of the 1860 presidential election are shown on this map. The states that Lincoln won are shaded red. Lincoln received more votes than any other candidate, although fewer than half of the voters supported him. However, he won the majority of the electoral college votes.

On December 20, 1860, South Carolina became the first state to secede from the United States. Mississippi, Alabama, Georgia, Texas, Florida, and Louisiana left the Union within two months. President James Buchanan declared in his last days in office that the federal government would not fight to prevent secession. Representatives from the seceded states drew up a constitution forming the Confederate States of America. The Confederacy also seized forts and arsenals belonging to the United States. Upon his inauguration on March 4, 1861, Lincoln became president of a country that faced the most daunting crisis of its existence.

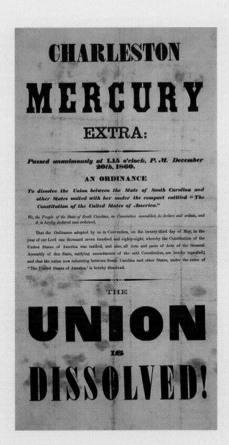

This December 20, 1860, edition of the *Charleston Mercury* announces South Carolina's vote to secede from the United States. The vote was made unanimously by a 169-member delegation at a convention called to discuss the issue.

The Civil War

Unlike Buchanan, the new president was not willing to allow the states in the South to secede peacefully. Lincoln did not wish to attack the Confederate forces, but he fully intended to defend government buildings and properties in the South. "You can have no conflict, without being yourselves the aggressors. You have no oath registered in Heaven to destroy the government, while I shall have the most solemn one to 'preserve, protect and defend' it," he told the South in his inaugural address.

The Confederacy eventually fired the first shots of the Civil War, bombarding a Union garrison protecting Fort Sumter in South Carolina on April 12, 1861. Southern forces captured the fort two days later. Lincoln condemned the attack, asking the remaining states to provide 75,000 militiamen to protect the Union. Virginia, Tennessee, North Carolina, and Arkansas then left the Union to join the Confederacy.

The time had come for people loyal to the Union to band together. Lincoln needed help in convincing the western states to send men. He asked his old rival Stephen Douglas, who had condemned the secessionists, to tour the West and help gather support. Though he had worked without stopping since the election, Douglas gladly obliged the president and set off to rally the western states.

The trip soon took a toll on Douglas and he fell gravely ill. Douglas died of typhoid on June 3, 1861.

Lincoln, determined to bring the nation back together, sent his armies into battle in the South. Enthusiasm ran high in the first few months, when many believed the war would end within the year. Several early stunning defeats of the Union army soon dampened the spirits of the soldiers and the public. People who had at first supported the war began clamoring for it to end and called on Lincoln to let the Confederacy leave the Union.

The End of Slavery

Lincoln recognized that he needed to offer the American people a convincing reason that they should continue to support the war effort. Many believed that it would be better to allow Confederate independence than to continue losing lives. Politically, Lincoln needed a moral justification for continuing the war.

As the Union armies advanced into the states of the Confederacy, African American slaves fled the plantations, asking to be allowed to fight for their freedom. Abolitionists had been encouraging Lincoln to end the practice of slavery, and the president began considering its restriction and possible elimination. With Lincoln's encouragement, Congress passed a law on March 13, 1862, forbidding the return of escaped slaves to their masters. On June 19, 1862, Congress finally passed legislation outlawing slavery in the territories, one of the goals that Lincoln put forth while debating Douglas.

Lincoln himself finally spoke out in support of abolition on September 22, 1862. In his speech he announced that in 100 days he would free any slaves in states rebelling against the Union at that time. True to his word, Lincoln issued the Emancipation Proclamation on January 1, 1863. The proclamation freed more than 3 million slaves

In addition to freeing slaves in the Confederate states, the Emancipation Proclamation *(right)* officially allowed black men to join the Union army and navy. The majority of the 186,000 black Union soldiers during the Civil War were escaped slaves from the South. At top is a photograph of members of the 107th U.S. Colored Infantry. It was taken sometime during the Civil War.

This broadside announces a $100,000 reward for the capture of John H. Surratt, John Wilkes Booth, and David E. Herold, who conspired to assassinate President Abraham Lincoln. Booth was the triggerman.

throughout the Confederacy. Americans now viewed supporters of the Confederacy as supporters of slavery. The armies of the North were now fighting not just to hold the Union together but to end slavery.

The Civil War lasted for four years. On April 9, 1865, Confederate general Robert E. Lee surrendered his Army of Northern Virginia to Union general Ulysses S. Grant. Abraham Lincoln did not live to see the war draw to a full end. On April 14, 1865, the actor John Wilkes Booth assassinated Lincoln at Ford's Theatre in Washington, D.C. By June of that year, all of the sizable Confederate armies had surrendered. On December 18, 1865, Congress passed the Thirteenth Amendment to the Constitution, forever abolishing slavery.

The Lincoln-Douglas Debates in History

The Senate campaign between Stephen Douglas and Abraham Lincoln changed the way politicians campaigned for voters. Today, debates between candidates are common in any election year. But before the

Lincoln-Douglas debates, political rivals never faced each other during a campaign. In an age without television, the debates reached millions of people across the nation. Americans witnessed them in person, read of them in newspapers, or bought them in book form. Today, the Lincoln-Douglas debates are held as a model for how a political argument should be carried out.

Even as the Lincoln-Douglas debates set a historical precedent in politics, they changed the course of the nation. Before the debates, Stephen Douglas seemed a likely victor in the 1860 presidential race. Abraham Lincoln's challenge cost Douglas the support of the Southern Democrats and perhaps the White House. The debates helped propel Lincoln into the presidency. If Lincoln had lost his presidential bid, the government would probably not have taken any kind of quick action toward abolishing slavery. Ultimately, the debates forced the nation to confront the slavery issue over the course of four bloody years and at a cost of more than 600,000 lives.

During the debates, Lincoln and Douglas took different stands on how to deal with slavery. They remained bitter political rivals through the election of 1860. The two men eventually found themselves on the same side, trying to reunite a divided nation.

Excerpt from Stephen Douglas's Speech in the Final Debate at Alton

But the Abolition party really think that under the Declaration of Independence the negro is equal to the white man, and that negro equality is an inalienable right conferred by the Almighty, and hence that all human laws in violation of it are null and void. With such men it is no use for me to argue. I hold that the signers of the Declaration of Independence had no reference to negroes at all when they declared all men to be created equal. They did not mean negro, nor the savage Indians, nor the Fejee Islanders, nor any other barbarous race. They were speaking of white men. They alluded to men of European birth and European descent,—to white men, and to none others,—when they declared that doctrine. I hold that this Government was established on the white basis. It was established by white men for the benefit of white men and their posterity forever, and should be administered by white men, and none others. But it does not follow, by any means, that merely because the negro is not a citizen, and merely because he is not our equal, that, therefore, he should be a slave. On the contrary it does follow that we ought to extend to the negro race, and to all other dependent races, all the rights, all the privileges, and all the immunities which they can exercise consistently with the safety of society. Humanity requires that we should give them all these privileges; Christianity commands that we should extend those privileges to them. The question then arises, what are those privileges, and what is the nature and extent of them. My answer is, that that is a question which each State must answer for itself . . . If the people of all the States will act on that great principle, and each State mind its own business, attend to its own affairs, take care of its own negroes, and not meddle with its neighbors, then there will be peace between the North and the South, the East and the West, throughout the whole Union.

Why can we not thus have peace? Why should we thus allow a sectional party to agitate this country, to array the North against the South, and convert us into enemies instead of friends, merely that a few ambitious men may ride into power on a sectional hobby? How long is it since these ambitious Northern men wished for a sectional organization? Did any one of them dream of a sectional party as long as the North was the weaker section and the South the stronger? Then all were opposed to sectional parties; but the moment the North obtained the majority in the House and Senate by the admission of California, and could elect a President without the aid of Southern votes, that moment ambitious Northern men formed a scheme to excite the North against the South, and make the people be governed in their votes by geographical lines, thinking that the North, being the stronger section, would outvote the South, and consequently they, the leaders, would ride into office on a sectional hobby.

Excerpt from Abraham Lincoln's Speech During the Final Debate at Alton

I have stated upon former occasions, and I may as well state again, what I understand to be the real issue in this controversy between Judge Douglas and myself. On the point of my wanting to make war between the Free and the Slave States, there has been no issue between us. So, too, when he assumes that I am in favor of introducing a perfect social and political equality between the white and black races. These are false issues, upon which Judge Douglas has tried to force the controversy. There is no foundation in truth for the charge that I maintain either of these propositions. The real issue in this controversy—the one pressing upon every mind—is the sentiment on the part of one class that looks upon the institution of slavery as a wrong, and of another class that does not look upon it as a wrong. The sentiment that contemplates the institution of slavery in this country as a wrong is the sentiment of the Republican party. It is the sentiment around which all their actions, all their arguments, circle, from which all their propositions radiate. They look upon it as being a moral, social, and political wrong; and while they contemplate it as such, they nevertheless have due regard for its actual existence among us, and the difficulties of getting rid of it in any satisfactory way and to all the constitutional obligations thrown about it. Yet, having a due regard for these, they desire a policy in regard to it that looks to its not creating any more danger. They insist that it should, as far as may be, be treated as a wrong; and one of the methods of treating it as a wrong is to make provision that it shall grow no larger. They also desire a policy that looks to a peaceful end of slavery at some time, as being wrong. These are the views they entertain in regard to it as I understand them; and all their sentiments, all their arguments and propositions, are brought within this range. I have said, and I repeat it here, that if there be a man amongst us who does not think that the institution of slavery is wrong in any one of the aspects of which I have spoken, he is misplaced, and ought not to be with us. And if there be a man amongst us who is so impatient of it as a wrong as to disregard its actual presence among us and the difficulty of getting rid of it suddenly in a satisfactory way, and to disregard the constitutional obligations thrown about it, that man is misplaced if he is on our platform. We disclaim sympathy with him in practical action. He is not placed properly with us . . .

That is the real issue. That is the issue that will continue in this country when these poor tongues of Judge Douglas and myself shall be silent. It is the eternal struggle between these two principles—right and wrong—throughout the world. They are the two principles that have stood face to face from the beginning of time, and will ever continue to struggle. The one is the common right of humanity, and the other the divine right of kings. It is the same principle in whatever shape it develops itself. It is the same spirit that says, "You work and toil and earn bread, and I'll eat it." No matter in what shape it comes, whether from the mouth of a king who seeks to bestride the people of his own nation and live by the fruit of their labor, or from one race of men as an apology for enslaving another race, it is the same tyrannical principle. I was glad to express my gratitude at Quincy, and I re-express it here, to Judge Douglas,—that he looks to no end of the institution of slavery. That will help the people to see where the struggle really is. It will hereafter place with us all men who really do wish the wrong may have an end. And whenever we can get rid of the fog which obscures the real question, when we can get Judge Douglas and his friends to avow a policy looking to its perpetuation,—we can get from among that class of men and bring them to the side of those who treat it as a wrong. Then there will soon be an end of it, and that end will be its "ultimate extinction." Whenever the issue can be distinctly made, and all extraneous matter thrown out so that men can fairly see the real difference between the parties, this controversy will soon be settled, and it will be done peaceably too. There will be no war, no violence. It will be placed again where the wisest and best men of the world placed it . . . I now say that, willingly or unwillingly, purposely or without purpose, Judge Douglas has been the most prominent instrument in changing the position of the institution of slavery which the fathers of the Government expected to come to an end ere this, . . . placing it where he openly confesses he has no desire there shall ever be an end of it.

— **1619** Africans first arrive in the American colonies as indentured servants.

— **1777** Vermont becomes the first state to ban slavery.

— **1808** The African slave trade ends.

— **1820** The Missouri Compromise is passed.

— **1847** Stephen Douglas becomes a senator representing Illinois.

— **1847** Abraham Lincoln is elected to the U.S. House of Representatives.

— **1850** The U.S. Senate passes the Compromise of 1850.

— **1854** Congress passes Douglas's Kansas-Nebraska Act, allowing individual territories to decide whether to allow slavery.

— **1856** Lincoln joins the Republican Party.

— **1857** The U.S. Supreme Court hands down its *Dred Scott* decision.

— **1858**   Lincoln and Douglas meet for seven debates while campaigning for the Senate.

— **1859**   The Illinois State Legislature reelects Douglas to the Senate.

— **1859**   Lincoln compiles the debates in a book.

— **1860**   Lincoln wins the presidential election, prompting eleven states to secede from the Union.

— **1861**   The Civil War begins.

— **1861**   Douglas dies while campaigning to drum up support for the Union.

— **1863**   Lincoln issues the Emancipation Proclamation, freeing all slaves in the Confederate states.

— **1865**   Actor John Wilkes Booth assassinates President Lincoln.

— **1865**   The Civil War ends.

— **1865**   The Thirteenth Amendment to the Constitution bans slavery in the United States.

GLOSSARY

advocate To argue in favor of a cause or proposal.

assassinate To kill, especially for political reasons.

bamboozelling (spelled "bamboozling" in contemporary English) Deceiving.

campaign Political operations preceding an election.

conspiracy A plot to carry out some harmful or illegal act.

demogogue (spelled "demagogue" in contemporary English) A speaker who appeals to the emotions and prejudices of his or her audience.

doctrine A principle or body of principles accepted as authoritative by some group or school.

emancipation Freedom from bondage.

flummox To confuse.

immigrant A person who enters and permanently settles in a foreign country.

implore To beg for urgently.

incumbent The person currently holding an office, especially a political one.

legislation A proposed or enacted law or group of laws.

legislature A body of lawmakers.

plantation A large agricultural estate.

secede To formally withdraw from an organization.

subvert To undermine.

territory An area dependent on and under the control of a governmental authority.

typhoid An infectious intestinal disease caused by contaminated food or water.

FOR MORE INFORMATION

The Abraham Lincoln Association
Old State Capitol
Springfield, IL 62701
Web site: http://www.alincolnassoc.com

Abraham Lincoln Papers at the Library of Congress
Manuscript Division
Library of Congress
101 Independence Avenue SE
Washington, DC 20540-4680
(202) 707-5387

The National Civil War Museum
One Lincoln Circle at Reservoir Park
P.O. Box 1861
Harrisburg, PA 17105
(866) 258-4729
Web site: http://www.nationalcivilwarmuseum.org

Web Sites

Due to the changing nature of Internet links, the Rosen Publishing Group, Inc., has developed an online list of Web sites related to the subject of this book. This site is updated regularly. Please use this link to access the list:

http://www.rosenlinks.com/ghds/ldsd

FOR FURTHER READING

Altman, Linda Jacobs. *Slavery and Abolition in American History*. Berkley Heights, NJ: Enslow Publishers, Inc, 1999.

Golay, Michael. *America at War: The Civil War*. New York: Facts on File, Inc., 1992.

Holzer, Harold, ed. *Lincoln—The Writer: A Treasury of His Greatest Speeches and Letters*. Honesdale, PA: Boyd's Mill Press, 2000.

Nolan, Jeanette Covert. *The Little Giant, Stephen A. Douglas*. New York: Simon & Schuster, 1964.

Tackach, James. *The Emancipation Proclamation: Abolishing Slavery in the South*. San Diego: Lucent Books, 1999.

BIBLIOGRAPHY

Donald, David Herbert. *Lincoln*. New York: Simon & Schuster, 1995.

Fehrenbacher, Don. E., ed. *Abraham Lincoln Speeches and Writings 1832–1858*. New York: Library of America, 1989.

Holzer, Harold, ed. *The Lincoln-Douglas Debates: The First Complete, Unexpurgiated Text*. New York: HarperCollins Publishers, 1993.

Jaffa, Harry V. *Crisis of the House Divided: An Interpretation of the Issues in the Lincoln-Douglas Debates*. New York: Doubleday and Company, Inc., 1959.

Johannsen, Robert W. *Stephen A. Douglas*. Urbana, IL: University of Illinois Press, 1997.

Nevins, Allan. *The Emergence of Lincoln, Vol. 1: Douglas, Buchanan, and Party Chaos, 1857–1859*. New York: Scribner, 1950.

Oates, Stephen B. *The Approaching Fury: Voices of the Storm, 1820–1861*. New York: HarperCollins Publishers, 1997.

Oliver, Robert Tarbell. *History of Public Speaking in America*. Boston: Allyn and Bacon, Inc., 1965.

Potter, David M., and Don E. Fehrenbacher. *The Impending Crisis, 1848–1861*. New York: Harper & Row, 1976.

Stampp, Kenneth M. *America in 1857: A Nation on the Brink*. New York: Oxford University Press, 1990.

Stephenson, Nathaniel W. *Abraham Lincoln and the Union*. New Haven, CT: Yale University Press, 1918.

Zarefsky, David. *Lincoln, Douglas, and Slavery: In the Crucible of Public Debate*. Chicago: The University of Chicago Press, 1990.

PRIMARY SOURCE IMAGE LIST

Page 4 (left): Photograph of Abraham Lincoln, taken by Mathew B. Brady on February 27, 1860. Housed at the Library of Congress Prints and Photographs Division in Washington, D.C.

Page 4 (right): Photograph of Stephen Douglas, taken between 1855 and 1861. Housed at the Library of Congress Prints and Photographs Division in Washington, D.C.

Page 8: Map of the United States, 1857, engraved by W. & A. K. Johnston. Housed at the Library of Congress Geography and Map Division in Washington, D.C.

Page 10 (right): Photograph of Stephen Douglas, taken between 1844 and 1860. Housed at the Library of Congress Prints and Photographs Division in Washington, D.C.

Page 11: An Act to Organize the Territories of Nebraska and Kansas, 1854. Housed at the National Archives in Washington, D.C.

Page 12 (top): Photograph of Abraham Lincoln, taken by Nicholas H. Shepherd around 1847. Housed at the Library of Congress Prints and Photographs Division in Washington, D.C.

Page 12 (bottom): Whig campaign handbill, 1846.

Page 17: July 31, 1858, letter from Abraham Lincoln to Stephen Douglas.

Page 21: Photograph of James Buchanan, taken between 1861 and 1865. Housed at the U.S. National Archives & Records Administration in Washington, D.C.

Page 22: Photograph of Lyman Trumbull, taken between 1860 and 1875. Housed at the Library of Congress Prints and Photographs Division in Washington, D.C.

Page 23: The *Lincoln and Douglas Meeting at Galesburg, Illinois, October 7, 1858*, illustration, published in *McClure's Magazine* in 1858. Housed at the New York Public Library.

Page 25: *Forcing Slavery down the Throat of a Freesoiler*, 1856 cartoon by John L. Magee. Housed at the Library of Congress Prints and Photographs Division in Washington, D.C.

Page 32: Anti-Lincoln political poster, published in 1858.

Page 36: Pages from Abraham Lincoln's scrapbook of his debates with Stephen Douglas, 1858. Housed at the Library of Congress Rare Book and Special Collections Division in Washington, D.C.

Page 39: September 10, 1859, letter from Joseph Medill to Abraham Lincoln. Housed at the Library of Congress in Washington, D.C.

Page 40: *Political Debates Between Hon. Abraham Lincoln and Hon. Stephen A. Douglas, in the Celebrated Campaign of 1858, in Illinois*, published in 1860. The Joseph Nathonson Collection of Lincolniana, McGill University.

Page 43: Photograph of campaign banner for Abraham Lincoln, 1860. Housed at the Library of Congress Prints and Photographs Division in Washington, D.C.

Page 46: "The Union is Dissolved!" published in the *Charleston Mercury* on December 20, 1860. Housed at the Library of Congress Rare Books and Special Collections Division, in Washington, D.C.

Page 48 (top): Photograph of the 107th U.S. Colored Infantry, taken between 1863 and 1865.

Page 48 (bottom): The Emancipation Proclamation, January 1, 1863. Housed at the National Archives in Washington, D.C.

Page 49: Reward poster for the capture of Lincoln's assassination conspirators, 1865. Housed at the Library of Congress Rare Book and Special Collections Division in Washington, D.C.

INDEX

About the Author

Jason Porterfield is a freelance writer who lives in Chicago.

Photo Credits

Design: Les Kanturek; **Editor:** Wayne Anderson